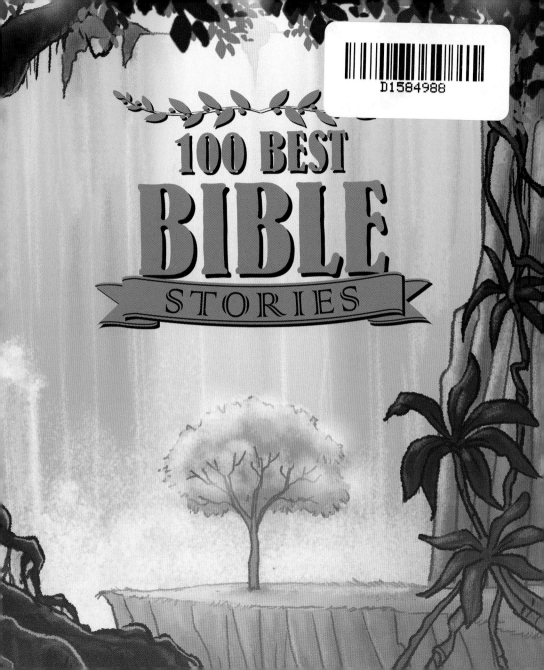

100 BEST
BIBLE
STORIES

100 Best Bible Stories

1st edition, 1st print
Copyright © Scandinavia Publishing House 2014
Drejervej 15, 3. DK-2400 Copenhagen NV, Denmark
info@sph.as • www.sph.as

Text: L. M. Alex • Editor: Cecilie Fodor
Illustrations: Gustavo Mazali
Graphic Design: Isabelle Gao & Hanyu Gao

Printed in China • ISBN: 9788771326604

This edition published by CLC International (UK), 2017
Bringing glory to God by making Christian literature
available to all nations so that people may come
to faith and maturity in the Lord Jesus Christ.
www.clc.org.uk

100 BEST
BIBLE
STORIES

Stories retold by L. M. Alex
Illustrations by Gustavo Mazali

SCANDINAVIA

Contents

Contents

THE OLD TESTAMENT

The First Day

Genesis 1:1-5

It was all about to begin. There was not yet an earth. There was not yet a sun or a moon. In every place . . . in every space . . . all was as dark as can be. But even in darkness, God was there. And God had a plan. "Let there be light!" said God. And there was light. Across all of space, it shined the rays of God's good love.

God Creates the World

Genesis 1:6-13

God was making the world. It was day number two. God made the heavens, and God made the earth. In between them was the wide, open sky. Now there was night, and there was day. Now there was heaven, and there was earth. On day three, God made the seas. He called for land to rise up from the water. "Let there be grass," said God. "Let there be plants and trees." Each had seeds for making more. So the earth began to grow with living things. God looked at what He had made and saw it was good.

The Sun and Moon

Genesis 1:14-19

It was day four. God filled the sky with stars to give light to the earth during nighttime. The biggest light of all would shine for day. This was the sun. Another would shine at night. This light was the moon. God looked out over all He had made. And God knew that it was good.

God Makes the Fishes, Birds, and Animals

Genesis 1:20-26

The world was about to come alive. God said, "Let the sea fill with fish. Let the sky fill with birds." God made mighty whales and tiny birds. Next, God made animals. Some to walk and some to slither. Some to creep and some to swing from high above. Last of all, God made people. He made man and woman so they were like Him. Of all the fish of the sea and the birds of the sky, the animals that walked and the animals that crept, it was people who were going to be the ones in charge. God smiled on all that He had made.

Life Begins

Genesis 2:1-7

It was day number seven. God was done making the world. He had filled it full of wonders . . . with the sea, the sun, plants, and animals. Now, it was time to rest. God blessed the seventh day. In the garden the animals were running around and the grass and plants were growing. The trees were stretching their branches to the sky and the rivers ran, bubbling with life. A man and a woman were waking up, too. It was Adam and Eve. They opened their eyes for the very first time. And they saw what a wonderful world God had made.

The Garden

Genesis 2:8–3:24

Adam and Eve lived in the Garden of Eden. It was a wonderful place full of animals and plants and good things to eat. There was just one rule. God said, "No eating from the tree at the middle of the garden." One day, Adam and Eve got curious. Why was this tree so special? They tasted the fruit . . . not bad at all! Yet God can see all things, and God was so sad. He told them they had to leave the perfect garden. From now on, Adam and Eve would work for their food. Even still, God would watch over them. Even still, God would love them very much.

The Very First Children

Genesis 4:1-7

God is never done with giving surprises. Soon enough, Eve had a belly that was big and round. Little baby Cain was born as a gift from God. Then came a brother named Abel. Adam and Eve were full of joy for their two small sons. God sure was good. The two boys grew and grew. Like all children, each one was special. Each one had something they were good at. Cain became the farmer while Abel watched the sheep.

Two Brothers

Genesis 4:8-17

Abel walked around with a big, happy smile. Cain was starting to worry. Did God love his brother more than him? Cain got more and more jealous until one day when Cain killed his brother. Then he tried to hide the truth. God knows every secret, of course. And He knew just what it was that Cain had done. God sent him away to wander in the desert alone. How very sorry he was. Cain prayed, and God was listening. God said He would keep Cain safe, and one day, Cain would have a family of his own.

Noah Builds a Boat

Genesis 6:1-22; 7:1-16

Families began to grow. People moved to new lands. But people were
starting to forget about God. They no longer listened to hear God's voice.
One man was different. His name was Noah. Noah loved God with all his
heart. So when God told him to build a boat, Noah obeyed. Noah built
a big and sturdy boat. God told him to fill the boat with animals, two by
two. Noah's family found two of each animal and put them on the boat.
Then Noah's family went in, and God shut the door. Then it began to rain;
water was falling from the sky! Soon, water rose around the boat.

A Sea without End

Genesis 7:17-8:8

It rained, and it rained, and it rained. For forty days and nights, the earth filled with water. The rivers and lakes got wider and wider until there was no ground left. Then even the mountains were covered by the sea. At last, all was still. Noah peeked out. The rain had stopped. Yet now they floated on a wide, open sea. Was there any place for the boat to land? Noah would send a bird to go find out. He took one of the doves and set it free. The dove came back to the boat. It had not found any place to land.

Boat on a Mountain

Genesis 8:10-19

Noah tried again. He took the dove and set it free. Again, the dove came back. But this time, the dove had a green leaf in its beak. The dove had found land. *Thump*, went the boat. They had landed on a rock. From there, they could see the water get lower and lower and lower. "It is time," God told Noah. The doors of the boat were opened. Out came the animals. At last, they were on dry land again . . . in a world that was beautiful and new.

The Promise in a Rainbow

Genesis 9:8-17

God's love was all around them in the fresh buds of spring. Noah lifted his face to the sun with gladness. There in the sky was a thing that no one had ever seen before. Stripes of every lovely color curved over the earth. Had there ever been anything so beautiful? "This is a rainbow," said God. "I made it so that all would know this promise that I will never flood the earth again."

The Tower of Babel

Genesis 11:1-9

One brick, two bricks, three bricks, four. The people had begun to build.
They were making a tower to reach to Heaven. God saw what they were
doing. The people didn't remember God, and He did not like it at all. But
God had just the way to stop them. The builders stood still in surprise.
"What was going on?" they thought. All of a sudden, each person was
babbling in a new language. No one could understand what his friends were
saying. No one could help each other. No one could build. They took one
last, sad look at their tower. Then, everyone went home.

On the Road

Genesis 12:1-9

Abraham and Sarah trusted God. So when God said to leave their home and family behind, they left it all. They knew God would keep them safe. Abraham and Sarah now lived in a tent. They did not get sad if others were mean. They could always move their tent somewhere else. It might be nice to have a real house and to have children. Yet Abraham and Sarah knew that God was taking care of them. So whatever they might miss, they stayed glad. And that made God glad, too.

A Promise in the Stars

Genesis 15:1-6

It was a night with no clouds in the sky. "The stars have never looked so bright," Abraham thought. Then, a gentle voice spoke. "Do you see all these stars?" said God. Abraham looked up. Some of the stars sparkled more than others. But each star was like a tiny, glittery jewel. "One day," said God, "your family will be as many as these stars." Abraham looked across the sky with wide eyes. He still did not even have a single child, but he trusted God's promise.

The Colorful Coat

Genesis 37:1-11

Abraham had a son named Isaac, who had a son named Jacob. Jacob had twelve fine sons. Next to last was Joseph. One day, Jacob called to Joseph. Jacob had a present for his son. It was a coat, a wonderful coat of many colors. Joseph could see his father loved him very much. The coat made his brothers feel angry. Why did only Joseph get a coat? One morning, Joseph burst out of bed. He ran to tell his family what he dreamed. "One day you will all come and bow to me and I will be your ruler," Joseph said. His brothers glared back.

A Far Away Land

Genesis 37:19-28; 39:1

The brothers had grown sick of hearing Joseph act so proud. They stuck him in a pit. Just then, some travelers were going by on their way to Egypt. His brothers pulled Joseph out of the pit. Did the travelers have room for a pesky little brother? So Joseph went to Egypt. Poor Joseph had lost it all. Yet he decided to be brave. He knew that God would be with him. And Joseph was right. Soon he got a job. Joseph would be a servant to someone rich and important.

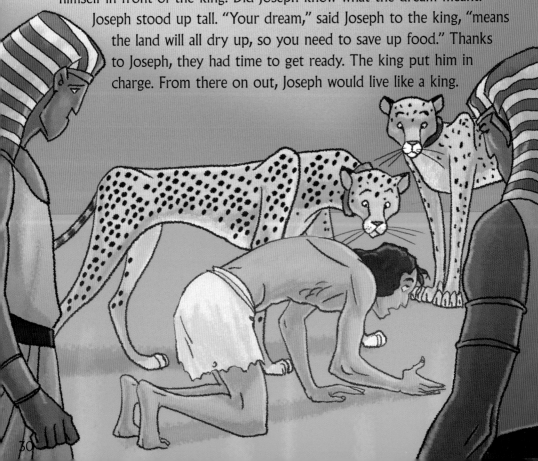

Joseph and the King

Genesis 39:2-40:15; 41:1-45

The lady of his master's house had told a lie that sent Joseph straight to jail. But Joseph stayed brave. God was with him even in jail. He would help the others in the jail. He would tell them about their dreams. Once, the king was feeling glum. He had dreamed a funny dream, and no one could tell him what it meant. Just then, the cupbearer spoke up. There was a man in the jail who knew about dreams. *Creak* went the jail door. Joseph found himself in front of the king. Did Joseph know what the dream meant?

Joseph stood up tall. "Your dream," said Joseph to the king, "means the land will all dry up, so you need to save up food." Thanks to Joseph, they had time to get ready. The king put him in charge. From there on out, Joseph would live like a king.

Joseph's Secret

Genesis 42:1-43:29; 45:1-15

The palace had visitors. Some men from far away wanted to buy food.
Joseph looked at the men. These were his brothers! Every one of them
were there—except for Benjamin, Joseph's only little brother. Of course
Joseph would help. But Benjamin had stayed at home. And Joseph wanted
to see his little brother very much. So he ordered his brothers to go get
Benjamin. Joseph burst with joy when he saw him. He was ready to tell the
truth. He was Joseph, their own brother!

The Family Together

Genesis 45:16-47:12

Joseph forgave his brothers. He asked them to come and live in the best part of Egypt, a place called Goshen. Their father could come along too, of course. So the family packed up and moved to Egypt. They would all be back together again in a land where Joseph was like a king with plenty of food and gladness as long as they lived.

A Land Gone Bad

Exodus 1:1-14

Many years later after Joseph had died, the family of Israel grew and grew. It made the new Egyptian king worry. What if this family tried to take charge? The king made a plan. He would make them all be slaves. Now the people of Israel could not get high and mighty. They would work hard all day long—or else. The sun was hot. The guards were mean. The slaves prayed to God for help. And God, of course, was listening.

A Baby in a Basket

Exodus 2:1-10

Miriam loved her baby brother. She wanted him safe from the wicked king. When Moses' mother put him in a basket in the river, Miriam watched him closely. Then—along came the princess to take her bath. Miriam sent the basket down the river. "Look!" cried the princess. "A baby in a basket. I think I will adopt him," she said. Miriam's plan had worked! No one would harm the baby of a princess. Miriam told the princess she could get a nanny for the baby, and she brought back their mom to take care of baby Moses.

The Run Away

Exodus 2:11-21

Moses was all grown up, and he was upset that the king was so mean to the people of Israel. The king found out and didn't want Moses there anymore, so Moses fled. At last, he rested. What was he going to do now? Some sisters came along to water their sheep. Moses was kind. He helped the sisters water their sheep. "We met the nicest young man," the sisters told their father. And they would soon become Moses' new family.

The Burning Bush

Exodus 3:1-14

Moses was looking after the sheep when all of a sudden, a bush burst into fire! It was God telling Moses to listen up. "Go back to the palace," said God. He wanted Moses to free the Israelites from their slavery. Moses was not so sure. The king would not listen to anyone. Not to Moses . . . and not even to God. Yet God told Moses not to worry. "I will go with you," said God.

Face to Face

Exodus 5:1-15

The people of Israel were hurting. It was time for Moses to face the king. The king did not look glad to see him. But Moses did his best to be brave. God had a message, so Moses told the king, "Let my people go." But the king only laughed. "No one tells me what to do," said the king. "Why should I take orders from God?" Things got worse. Moses had made the king mad. So now the slaves had to work even more.

Ten Plagues

Exodus 7:10-12:32

The king did not care what anyone had to say. So God decided to send warnings. But the king would not listen. "Very well," Moses told him. The king would be punished. And God did just that. Finally, Moses gave the king one last warning. But the king did not listen, and when he woke up, his son had died. Now the king had enough. "Get out of here, Moses!" cried the king. "And take those slaves with you." The people of Israel were finally free.

The Exodus

Exodus 12:33-14:2

The people of Israel got ready in a hurry. They called their animals and packed as fast as they could. They would be gone before the sun had even come up. God showed them where to go using a tall cloud in the sky. They rested when they got to the sea. It was time to thank God. God had heard their prayers and set them free.

The Chase

Exodus 14:5-22

The Israelites were camping by the seaside when they looked up and could hardly believe what they saw. There was the whole Egyptian army coming after them! Pharaoh had decided to get his slaves back after all. But Moses had faith. He reached out his staff over the sea, and there the waves started to peel back on either side. The sea had split in two. A path of land had appeared. The Israelites hurried to safety on the other side of the sea.

Moses and the Law

Exodus 19:3-25

God called Moses up to the mountain top. God was going to give Moses the Law. From the ground below, the people saw a cloud swallow the mountain. Was Moses going to be okay? But down came Moses again, perfectly fine. "God was talking to Moses on that mountain," said the people. So they listened to all that Moses had heard from God.

Ten Commandments

Exodus 20:1-21

God gave Moses ten laws on stone tablets. "There will be no gods but Me,"
God said. He did not want the people praying to other gods. He wanted them
to love others, to not use curse words, and to keep one day a week as holy.
They must not kill, or cheat, or steal. They must not lie or wish for what was
not theirs. The people had seen the mountain shake when God was giving
Moses the Law. "Don't be afraid," Moses told them. God had given them laws
in order to help them.

Joshua Leads the People

Joshua 1:1-9

The desert was hot and dusty. The Israelites wanted to leave, but they waited on God. At last, God said it was time. Moses had died, and Joshua was the new leader. "Be strong," God told Joshua, "and be brave." Joshua was going to lead the people into their new land.

The Fall of Jericho

Joshua 6:1-20

Jericho was a city behind a high, strong wall. But no wall can keep out God. And God had decided to give the city to the people of Israel. God told their leader Joshua just what to do. Joshua marched the Israelites around the city. Around and around and around they went. They blew on their trumpets. Each gave a shout. Then as they watched, the walls of Jericho fell!

Gideon Wants to be Sure

Judges 6:36-40

Gideon was not sure. Would God please give him a sign? A sign to show Gideon that God had picked him to help His people. Gideon laid some wool down on the floor. The next morning, the wool was all wet while the ground was perfectly dry! It seemed like magic. Still, Gideon wanted to be extra, *extra* sure. Would God please switch them the next day? Sure enough, the wool kept dry while the ground got wet. *Okay then*, thought Gideon, *God wanted him, a farm boy, to be a warrior.*

A Warrior for God

Judges 7:1-25; 8:22-23

Gideon was ready to go and fight for God. "Not so fast," God said. He wanted the people to know that God was the one in charge. So, God told Gideon to send most of his soldiers home. Then, with just a tiny army, Gideon led them to battle, and God helped them win. Afterward, the people begged Gideon to be their king. But Gideon said, "It is God who shall be your King."

Samson the Strong

Judges 13:1-24

An angel told a woman she would have a son. When the baby came, his mother named him Samson. She did everything the angel told her to do. She fed him good, clean foods, but most importantly, she made sure to never cut his hair. His mother was careful to obey all the angel told her to do. Samson was blessed and grew big and strong and brave.

Samson and the Lion

Judges 14:5-6

Samson went for a walk one day. Suddenly—there stood a lion roaring right at him! Samson had no weapons to help him. But Samson was not afraid. God was there. Samson killed the lion using just his hands. Then he went on his way to find his parents. Yet Samson never bragged to anyone about what a mighty thing that he had done.

Samson's Last Stand

Judges 16:20-30

Samson's enemies asked his girlfriend Delilah to find out the secret to his strength. Samson told her, "I must never cut my hair." That night, Samson's hair was cut while he slept. His strength was no more. Samson had been tricked. And now he was in jail without the power to escape. One evening at a party, his enemies told Samson's guards, "Let's laugh at the man we once feared." So Samson was taken to the arena in his chains. Yet little did they know—Samson's hair had grown. Samson prayed to God, "May I have one last chance to be strong." Then Samson pushed the pillars and the arena fell to dust.

Ruth, the Good Servant

Ruth 1:1-2:18

Ruth lived in a foreign country. She tried to always do right. A famine came to the land, and Ruth's husband died. His mother Naomi told Ruth she may return to her homeland. But Ruth was not going to leave old Naomi by herself. Ruth worked hard to help Naomi and barely rested at all. She picked up scraps of grain in a field for them to eat. The owner of the field heard of Ruth's good deeds. After that, there was always free grain left for Ruth.

Ruth's New Beginning

Ruth 3:1-11; 4:9-17

Ruth had taken good care of Naomi. Naomi wanted Ruth to be cared for, too. She told Ruth, "The owner of the field likes you. Go and visit him." Ruth went to visit the owner of the field, named Boaz. It wasn't long before Ruth and Boaz were married. God blessed Ruth with a new family of her own because she had served Him by loving others.

The Shepherd

1 Samuel 16:1-13

The prophet Samuel visited Jesse in Bethlehem. God had chosen one of his sons to be king. Jesse was excited and called in his big, strong sons. Samuel looked them over and asked, "Are these all of your sons?" Jesse said, "Only David, who is watching the sheep, is left. But he's just a boy." Still, Samuel called for David. When Samuel saw the shepherd, he said, "He's the one!" Samuel gave David the blessing of a future king.

The Giant

1 Samuel 17:4-26

David's father told David to bring his older brothers their lunch. So, the shepherd boy went to where the soldiers were fighting. David arrived at the battlefield as a war cry rang out. He rushed to find his brothers among Israel's army. His brothers and all the soldiers looked terrified. The enemy had a giant named Goliath on their side! But David was not afraid. The boy said, "With our trust in God, why should we be afraid?"

David and Goliath

I Samuel 17:38-49

King Saul gave David a helmet, armor, and a sword. They were all too big and heavy for a boy though. So instead, David picked up five stones to fight with. Then with his slingshot in hand, David met the giant. Goliath glared down. He growled a ferocious growl. David picked a stone from his bag and spun his sling. KA-POW—the stone hit Goliath right in the head! The giant fell face down in the dirt. David had won.

A King, Good and True

2 Samuel 5:6-25

King David asked God for help in all he did, in where to go, and in how to rule. A king that would obey was a king that made God happy. David's family grew bigger. David's army grew stronger. The people could trust King David to do what was right, to do what was fair. Never was a land more mighty than David's. Never was a king more loved.

Solomon's Wish

1 Kings 2:10-12, 3:3-9

David was old and sick, so before he died he made his son Solomon the new king. Solomon gave thanks to God. One night God visited him in a dream. "Make a wish," God told Solomon, "for what you want most." Solomon said, "I am still so young. Help me to rule and to know what is fair. Make me wise—so that I know what is right and what is wrong." God gladly made Solomon the wisest king and also the richest king who ever lived.

A House for God

1 Kings 5:1-6:38

Wise Solomon made friends with Egypt and other lands far away. At last there was peace. King Solomon knew what it was time to do. "My father did not get to build what he dreamed of building," said Solomon to the people, "so now we are going to build it . . . a house for God." At last they would have a temple for worshiping God. Solomon grew wiser, richer, and more famous. He was remembered as the wisest king who ever lived.

Elijah and the Ravens

1 Kings 17:2-6

God loved his prophet Elijah, and Elijah loved God. Once Elijah was hiding out by a stream. He had water to drink, and God kept him safe. Suddenly, Elijah saw shadows on the ground. It was big, black birds—swooping right at him! What was it the birds dropped from their beaks? It was chunks of bread and meat. God had sent ravens to bring food for Elijah to eat. The birds brought food each day in the morning and night.

The Woman with Sticks

1 Kings 17:7-16

The stream where Elijah was dried up. God had a new plan. He sent Elijah into town. A poor woman was picking up sticks. Elijah asked her for some water and a little bread. The woman had no bread, only a bit of flour and oil. "Do not worry," Elijah told her. "Make some bread to share with me, and God will make sure you will not run out of flour or oil." The woman made lots of bread, and God kept her jars full.

Elijah's Goodbye

2 Kings 2:1-11

It was almost time for Elijah to go. One day, he was walking along with Elisha, his helper, when a ride came from heaven. It was horses pulling a chariot ablaze with fire! Then a big gust of wind whirled around them. The wind picked Elijah up, and he was gone. Elijah had been taken to heaven to be with God.

Call for a Queen

Esther 1:1-2:17

Esther lived in the land of Persia with her cousin. "Tell no one," he had said, "that we are from Israel." One day, a call came from the royal palace. The king of the land was looking for a queen. Royal servants gave each maiden one whole year of beauty treatment and served them special food, too. *Who is this beautiful maiden?* thought the king. When the king met Esther, his choice was made.

Esther Is Queen

Esther 2:17-18

No other maiden was like Esther, the king had decided. He put the royal crown on her head. Esther would be his wife. A great feast was held for the wedding of the king and Esther . . . now a queen.

The Queen's Secret

Esther 4:4-8:16

Queen Esther had just heard some terrible news. There was an order for the Israelite people to be killed. That meant Esther . . . and Esther's whole family! She had to do something. She decided to be very brave. When the king saw his lovely queen, his heart filled with love. "Ask for anything," he said. So Esther told him her secret. She was from Israel. Would the king help? Of course he would! Esther had saved her people the Israelites.

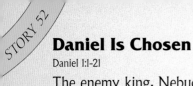

Daniel Is Chosen

Daniel 1:1-21

The enemy king, Nebuchadnezzar, had taken more of God's people captive. The king wanted the smartest and best of the young men to work for him. Daniel and his friends obeyed God's plan, and it made them the healthiest and smartest of all. So the king picked them to serve in his palace.

Writing on the Wall

Daniel 5:1-29

The king was having a feast when God came to visit. The guests looked up because writing had appeared on the wall! The king was very afraid. He called for Daniel. Daniel would be able to tell him what the letters said. The news was not good. God was angry. The king had been too busy having fun to be good. So now, God was going to make him pay. The sad king thanked Daniel for telling him the truth.

Daniel in the Lions' Den

Daniel 6:7-29

There was a new rule that said for one month no one could pray to God but only to the king. Well, that was not a rule Daniel was going to obey. The king loved Daniel, but rules were rules. Daniel would have to be thrown into the den of lions. Yet Daniel trusted in God. Sure enough, God shut the lions' mouths. The king peeked in. Daniel was safe and sound. "Let us pray to the one true God!" cried the king.

Jonah and the Whale

Jonah 1:1-17

God asked Jonah for his help to go and tell a city to stop doing bad things and to worship God. But Jonah ran away instead. He tried to sail across the sea to hide out in a land far away. God knew just where Jonah was and sent a mighty storm. The sailors were afraid, but Jonah asked them to throw him into the waters. When they did, the waters became calm. A whale then swallowed Jonah up where Jonah was safe inside.

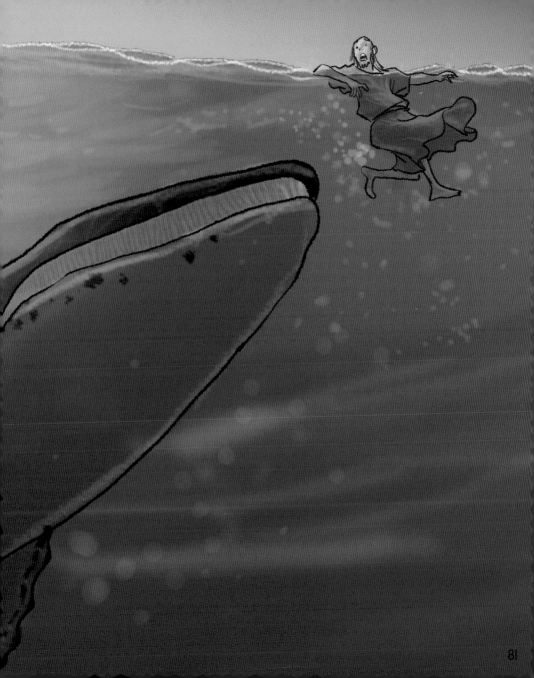

Jonah's Second Chance

Jonah 2-4

Inside the whale, Jonah prayed to God, "I was wrong to try and hide!" So God had the whale spit Jonah out. Then Jonah did what God asked and went to the city where the people did not know God. Jonah told them to stop doing wrong and to believe in God. The ruler and the people believed in God and were saved.

THE NEW TESTAMENT

Mary and the Angel

Luke 1:27-38

Mary was a young woman and not yet married. So when an angel visited, the message was surprising. "You are going to have a baby," said the angel to Mary. Mary said, "But how can I have a baby without a husband?" The angel answered, "The father of your baby is God. The baby shall be named Jesus, God's own Son." Mary trusted God. She was happy for the news. She told the angel, "May it happen just as you say."

Joseph's Visit

Matthew 1:20-25

The angel visited Joseph, who was soon to be Mary's husband. "Mary's baby is the Son of God," the angel said. "You shall name Him Jesus. He will save people from their sins." Joseph believed all the angel told him and prepared to be Jesus' dad here on earth.

The First Christmas

Luke 2:4-7

It was time. Jesus was ready to be born. Joseph led the donkey while Mary rode on its back. When they got to the inn, there was no more room. They would have to stay out with the animals instead. There in the animal stable, baby Jesus was born. Mary wrapped Him up with swaddling clothes. They laid Jesus in a manger that was used to hold hay. Then they looked at baby Jesus, overflowing with love.

Shepherds by Night

Luke 2:8-14

Some shepherds were watching their sheep one night when a light shone all around them. They were terrified. Then a voice said, "Fear not." It was an angel! "I bring you good news," said the angel. "Christ is born." Suddenly, there were even more angels there. The angels were praising God, saying, "Glory to God! Peace on earth. May good come to those with whom God is pleased." The shepherds watched the angels in amazement.

The Visitors

Luke 2:15-20

The angels who had visited the field went back to heaven. The shepherds looked at each other and said, "Let's go to Bethlehem and see this news for ourselves." Then they rushed to find Jesus. The shepherds found Mary and Joseph inside the stable. And there lay Jesus asleep on the hay in the manger. The shepherds could not wait to spread the exciting news. Then they praised God for all they had seen and heard.

Three Wise Men

Matthew 2:9-12

In a land far away, three wise men had seen a star. The star meant the one they were waiting for had come. Jesus had been born. Filled with joy, the three wise men headed out to find him. The star led them all the way to where Jesus was. When they saw the child, they knelt down to worship Him. They gave Him the gifts of treasure that they had carried. Then the three wise men went back home to the land far away, from where they had come.

A Boy Named Jesus

Luke 2:41-51

It was time to go home after their visit to Jerusalem. Joseph and Mary thought Jesus was right behind them. But when they looked, Jesus was nowhere to be seen. They rushed back and looked everywhere for the boy. There at last was Jesus talking to teachers and priests. He was teaching the teachers about the many things He knew. His mother cried, "We have looked everywhere for you!" But He answered, "Didn't you know I had to be in My father's house?"

The Baptism

Luke 1:11-25,56-80; Matthew 3:1-17

God gave Mary's cousin Elizabeth and Zechariah a baby in their old age. God told them that baby John would be special. "You are going to be a prophet," Zechariah told his son. "You will teach and give light to those in darkness." John grew up strong in spirit and close to God. He went to live in the desert until Jesus came to him to be baptized. When John baptized Jesus, God's voice said, "This is My beloved Son. I delight in Him."

The Call of Jesus

Mark 1:14-20

Jesus traveled from place to place telling people about the Kingdom of God. God was ready to welcome them to a life of peace and joy. All they had to do was believe and stop doing wrong. Soon Jesus saw some fishermen at work with their nets. Jesus said to them, "Follow Me and I'll show you how to catch people instead of fish." Each fisherman left his ship and followed after Jesus. Simon, Andrew, James, and John were now disciples.

The Wedding Feast

John 2:1-11

Jesus and His disciples were asked to come to a wedding. Mary was glad to see her son arrive. There was a problem. The wedding ran out of wine, but Mary knew Jesus could help. Jesus told the servants to fill all the pitchers with water. When the servants poured it out into the cups—the water had turned into wine! It was the best wine anyone had ever tasted. With that, the miracles of Jesus had now begun. Jesus showed His power, and His disciples believed in Him.

Jesus Heals

Luke 5:18-26

The friends of a sick man had a plan to get to Jesus. But the house was too full to get through the door. So, they sent their friend down through the roof. Very gently, they lowered the sick man into the house. Jesus was amazed—what good friends this man had! Jesus said, "Get up, take your mat and go home." And right away, the man was healed. The man got up and thanked God the whole way home. And everyone in the house knew that God was great.

Jesus on the Sea

Mark 4:35-38

It had been a long day in Galilee. Jesus had healed many, and Jesus had fed many. Now it was almost dark. Time to set sail. Jesus and His disciples got in their boat to cross the sea. A storm started to form over the water. But Jesus didn't worry. He knew that God was always with Him. So he just fell sound asleep on His pillow. The disciples were afraid though. How could Jesus be sleeping in a storm like this?

Jesus Stops the Storm

Mark 4:37-40

The storm was growing stronger and stronger. The waves crashed. The sky howled. The disciples no longer felt brave. They ran to wake Jesus. "Master," cried a disciple, "we are about to drown!" Jesus got up and went outside. "Peace, be still," said Jesus. Then the storm stopped. Everything grew calm and quiet. Jesus said to his disciples, "Why were you afraid?" Jesus knew God was there protecting them no matter what.

The Sick Girl

Mark 5:22-24, 35-39; Luke 8:40-42, 49-52

Jairus was an important man in town. Many of his friends didn't like Jesus, but Jairus respected Jesus and believed Jesus had power. One day Jairus' daughter became very sick. It was his only daughter and she was very, very ill. So Jairus went to find out if Jesus would help. Jesus agreed to help and got up to go with Jairus to his house. A servant ran out to meet Jesus and Jairus as they walked and said it was too late. Jairus' little daughter had already died. But Jesus said to Jairus, "Don't worry; only believe." Jesus and three disciples went into the house. Jesus looked down at the little girl and said, "She's not dead . . . only sleeping."

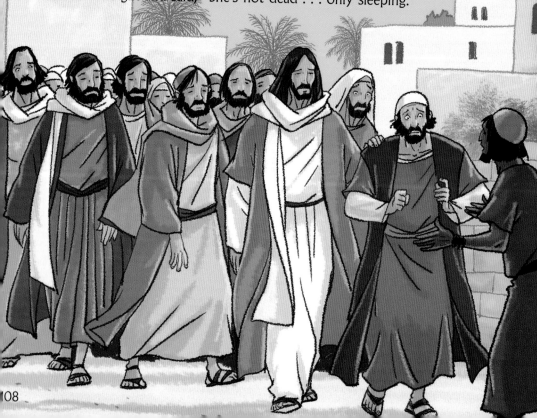

The Girl Awakes

Mark 5:39-42; Luke 8:49-55

The girl had died, but Jesus said she was just sleeping. *What was Jesus thinking?* the people thought. And now Jesus was looking down at the girl and taking her hand saying, "Little girl, get up." The girl's eyes fluttered. Then she sat straight up. Her family and friends could hardly believe their eyes! Jesus had brought the little girl back from the dead. Her father and mother thanked Jesus through tears of joy.

The Boy's Gift

Matthew 14:15-21

Jesus was teaching a crowd in the desert. It grew late. His friends said, "There is no food for the people to eat." Just then, a small boy stepped out of the crowd. "I have two fish and five loaves of bread," said the boy. Jesus took the boy's gift. Jesus prayed a blessing on it. Then He started to break the fish and bread in pieces. More and more, more and more. There was so much food that the whole crowd stuffed their bellies full!

Walking on Water

John 6:17-20

It was a dark and stormy night on the sea. The disciples wished Jesus was with them, but He was spending alone time on a mountain. They looked out across the dark, wild waves. Then they saw it, a man walking on the water! He was coming straight toward them. They were terrified. Then the man on the water spoke with a voice they knew. "Do not be afraid," said Jesus. "It is I."

Peter Steps Out

Matthew 14:28-32

The disciples were amazed to see Jesus walking on the sea. "If it's really you," said Peter, "then let me come out there." Jesus agreed, so Peter climbed over the edge of the boat. He stretched out his foot. Peter could walk on water too! Then Peter saw the storm all around him. He became afraid. Peter crashed down into the water. Jesus came to help. "Why did you not trust me?" said Jesus as He pulled Peter out. Jesus helped Peter onto the boat, and the storm stopped.

The Lost Coin

A Story Jesus Told. Luke 15:8-10

A woman had lost one of her ten special silver coins. She searched her house all over until she found it. Then she called her friends to celebrate the happy news. Like this, the angels celebrate each time a lost person believes in Jesus and says I'm sorry for making bad choices.

The Lost Son

A Story Jesus Told. Luke 15:10-20

A man had saved some money for his two sons to inherit. The younger son said, "Father, I want my money now." Then he left home and wasted all his money on stupid things. At last he ran out of money. The son started to get hungry. He went back home very, very sad because of all the foolish things he had done. Yet to his surprise, his father wasn't angry with him; he was just glad his son was home. And so it is with your Father in heaven. Turn away from doing wrong, and God will forgive you.

Lazarus Sleeps

John 11:7-25

One day Jesus said to his disciples, "Let's go to our friend Lazarus' house. Lazarus has died, but I am going to wake him up again." When they arrived, Lazarus had already been dead for four days. Jesus told Lazarus' sister Martha, "Your brother will wake up to life again." Martha answered, "I know he will rise to go to heaven." Jesus said, "Believe in Me, and even the dead will live."

117

Jesus Weeps

John 11:28-37

Martha's sister Mary learned that Jesus had come. She ran to see Him. "If you had been here," cried Mary, "then my brother Lazarus would not have died." Seeing Mary cry made Jesus terribly sad. Jesus asked to be taken to where Lazarus was. When He saw the grave of His good friend, Jesus cried. Some said, "Look how much Jesus loved Lazarus!" But others said, "Could Jesus not save his own friend?"

Lazarus Rises

John 11:38-44

Jesus was upset over the death of His friend Lazarus. He said to those at the grave, "Take the stone away." "But Lord," Martha said, "he's been dead for four days!" Jesus said to Martha, "Didn't I tell you to believe?" The grave stone was rolled away. Jesus prayed to God, thanking Him for the miracle God was about to do. Then Jesus cried out, "Lazarus, come out of there!" Lazarus rose up just as if he had never even been dead.

Jesus and the Children

Mark 10:13-16

Everyone wanted to get close to Jesus. They crowded around. The disciples tried to send all the children away, but Jesus stopped them. "Don't send them away! Let the children come to Me," said Jesus. He picked the children up in His arms, and He blessed them.

Zacchaeus in a Tree

Luke 19:1-5

Zacchaeus was very short. He was also very rich. Zacchaeus took money from others that was not his. One day Jesus came to Jericho. Everyone wanted to see Jesus—even tiny Zacchaeus. Zacchaeus had to climb up a tree in order to see. When Jesus walked by the tree, He stopped and looked up. "Zacchaeus, come down," said Jesus. "I'm coming to eat at your house today."

Lost and Found

Luke 19:6-10

Of all the people in Jericho, Jesus had picked Zacchaeus—a man whom everyone knew did wrong! Zacchaeus scrambled down the tree and ran to Jesus. He was filled with joy that Jesus wanted to be his friend. "Lord," said Zacchaeus, "I will give half my riches to the poor. And anything I stole, I will give the person back even more." Jesus could see Zacchaeus was sorry and forgave him.

The Road of Jesus

Matthew 21:8-11

Jesus was coming to Jerusalem! People from all around came to the road. They laid their clothes down for His donkey to walk on . . . just like anyone should do for a king. "Hosanna!" they cried, waving leaves from a palm tree. As Jesus came into Jerusalem, the city was curious. "Who is this?" they asked. The people who had followed after Jesus cried out, "It is Jesus, the prophet of Galilee!"

The Last Supper

John 14; Matthew 26:26-30

"It's almost time for Me to go," said Jesus at supper. His friends looked at one another with sad faces. "Yet still," Jesus told them, "I will be with you even when you can't see Me." Jesus broke bread for them to eat and then passed His cup for all to have a sip. "Keep My words inside your heart,"

Jesus said. "Then in your heart, I will always be." They ate their last bread together and sang a song. Then Jesus told them to stand. It was time for them to go, so God's will could be done.

Jesus in the Garden

Matthew 26:36-56

After supper, Jesus prayed in a garden. He and His friends were turning to go when they suddenly stopped. Men with swords were coming straight for Jesus. And who led the way but the disciple Judas. Peter, a friend of Jesus, drew his sword. "Put that away," Jesus ordered. "This is what must be," He said. Then the soldiers took Jesus, and He was gone.

The Rooster Crows

Matthew 26:31-35,69-75; John 18:15-27

"It can't be true," Peter had said. "I won't let them take you away."
But Jesus had told Peter that Peter would be afraid and lie saying
he didn't know Jesus. Jesus said, "Even before morning, when the
rooster crows you will have lied about knowing Me." Now Jesus
had been taken. Peter stood by a fire getting warm. "Hey you," said
a soldier. "I saw you with Jesus, right?" Peter answered, "Jesus? I
don't even know Him." Just then, *cock-a-doodle-doo!* The rooster
made Peter remember. Jesus had been right. Peter was too afraid to
act like a friend.

The Price for the World

Matthew 27:26-54

It had been decided. Jesus was going to be nailed to a cross. They stuck a crown of thorns on His head and put Him high on a hill. Jesus felt the hurt. He was bleeding, and His friends had gone away. Jesus felt alone. And He was going to die. But Jesus had decided to die all along. He was praying for the sins of the world to be forgiven. He was dying so that the world could be saved. Jesus looked up to God one last time then He shut His eyes.

Guards at the Cave

Matthew 27:62-66

Jesus had died the day before. Yet the teachers of the law were starting to worry. What was it Jesus had said . . . that He would rise from the dead? *Better to be safe than sorry*, thought the teachers. They made sure the cave was closed tight with a huge rock in front. Then they put soldiers to stand guard. "Who could get in or out of a cave like that?" said the teachers.

The Angel and the Stone

Luke 24:1-4; Matthew 28:1-4

Mary and Mary Magdalene woke up early. They were going to visit the cave where Jesus was buried. They headed out just as the sun was starting to rise. As they got to the cave, the ground started to shake. What was happening? It was an angel rolling away the giant rock that covered up the tomb. As the dust cleared, the women looked around. There lay the two guards, who had stood guard at the tomb and the angel was sitting on the rock.

135

Jesus Is Alive

Matthew 28:5-8; Luke 24:5-10

The angel's face shone like lightening. His clothes were white as snow. From his seat on the rock, the angel looked down at the women. "Don't be afraid," said the angel. "I know you came because of Jesus . . . but He is not here." The women listened as still as statues. The angel smiled. "Jesus is risen," he said. "Go see for yourself." Sure enough, no one was in the cave. The women felt full of fear and joy all at once! They ran to tell the news.

Jesus Appears

John 20:19-23

The disciples were waiting for a friend, a friend who had died. They were waiting for Jesus. The women had told them that Jesus was alive and well. All of a sudden, Jesus appeared and was standing among them. He said, "Peace be with you," and showed them the wounds on His hands and feet. The disciples were filled with joy to see Jesus again.

The Full Net

John 21:1-7

"Any luck?" yelled a man from the shore. The friends had been fishing all night but caught nothing. The man said to throw the net on the other side of the boat. Sure enough—the net was now filled with fish! Now they knew who this man was. It was Jesus on shore. When Peter realized this, he leaped into the water with a splash. Peter starting swimming to shore as fast as he could.

Into Heaven

Acts 1:6-11

Jesus came to visit His friends one last time. He wanted them to be His witnesses. So He told them to tell the good news of God in every corner of the world. Then He was lifted up in a cloud and they could no longer see Him. Two angels were standing on the mountain with the people who tried to catch one last glimpse of Jesus. The angels said, "Just like Jesus went up, He will come back again."

The Angel in Jail

Acts 5:12-42

The priests and teachers watched Peter and his friends with long frowns.
Were they still talking about Jesus after being told not to? "Throw them
in jail," said the priests and teachers. But an angel came at night and
opened the jail doors. He told them to keep teaching about Jesus. The next
morning the priests and teachers came to find the missing prisoners. They
found them still teaching about Jesus and healing sick people. Peter was no
longer afraid. "We must obey God over people," said Peter. He and the
apostles kept talking about Jesus to anyone who would listen.

Saul

Acts 9:1-6

The disciples who loved Jesus had a problem. Saul was on his way to put them in jail. But God came to the rescue. Saul was rushing down the road when a bright light shone around him. Saul fell down to the ground. He was very afraid. Then a voice from heaven spoke. "Why do you fight Me?" said Jesus. "Get up, and go to the city." There was something God wanted him to do. Saul obeyed. His servants had to lead him by the hand because Saul was now blind and couldn't see where he was going!

Saul the Saved

Acts 9:17-20

Saul was praying. He had been in the city now for three whole days. And still, Saul waited. Still, Saul could not see a thing. There in the darkness, Saul felt two hands touch him. Was this the man God told him to wait for? All of a sudden, Paul could see again . . . and there stood Ananias in front of him. Saul wanted to be baptized right away. Then Saul went to tell as many as he could about Jesus, the Son of God.

The Earthquake

Acts 16:23-26

Saul got a new name: Apostle Paul. He taught about Jesus in as many countries as he could go. He healed, and he baptized. And when Paul was put in jail, he stayed brave. He took the time to write letters to the churches that he had built. It was midnight in the jail when the prisoners heard singing. Paul and Silas were singing and praying to God. Suddenly the jail started to shake. The cell doors flew open. And the chains of all the prisoners fell to the floor.

The Prison Guard

Acts 16:26-34

The jail doors had flown open by just a prayer. The guard now trembled with fear. He bowed down in front of the two apostles. "Sirs!" said the guard. "What must I do to be saved?" Paul and Silas said that he just needed to believe in Jesus. They had wounds on their bodies, so the guard washed them and took them to his house for a meal. Then the guard and his whole family were baptized. The jailer was filled with joy because he and his whole family now believed in God.

The Shipwreck

Acts 28

Paul was once again in chains. He just couldn't stop talking about Jesus. He was taken onboard a ship headed for Rome, so he could be put in prison there. But out at sea, the boat got caught in a mighty storm. The ship ran aground, so they had to jump out into the water and swim to shore to an island. People at the island were friendly and brought them food. When Paul healed a sick man, the rest of the sick on the island came and were healed, too.